Silvia's Soccer Game

Written by Nancy Leber
Photographs by Elliott Smith

Today is the big soccer game.

Silvia meets the other Super Sports at the soccer field.

Are the Super Sports ready
for the Blue Stars?

The Super Sports have on their shorts and shirts.

Are the Super Sports ready
for the Blue Stars?

The Super Sports have on their shoes
and shin pads.

Are the Super Sports ready for
the Blue Stars?

The coach shows them one last shot.
The Super Sports are ready for
the Blue Stars.

The Super Sports run to the ball.
The Blue Stars run to the ball, too.

The Super Sports spin and kick.
The Blue Stars spin and kick, too.

Silvia stops the ball.

She wants to score.
The Blue Stars want to score, too.

Silvia shoots!

Silvia scores!

Silvia is ready for the Blue Stars!
And so are the Super Sports.